ia

1843–1905)

that the sun
of thy sway,
d creed obey,
of one …

unite
ne!

's might:
n red,
'o!

1887)

History Through Poetry
Victorians

Paul Dowswell

Iguanado
Professor Edward Forbes (1

A thousand age
His skele
But now his
And

His bone

W
HODDER
Wayland

an imprint of Hodder Children's Books

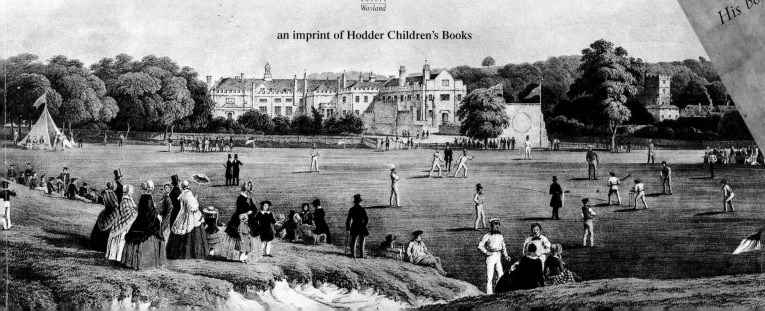

History Through Poetry
Tudors
Victorians

Editor: Jason Hook
Designer: Simon Borrough
Cover Concept: Richard Hook

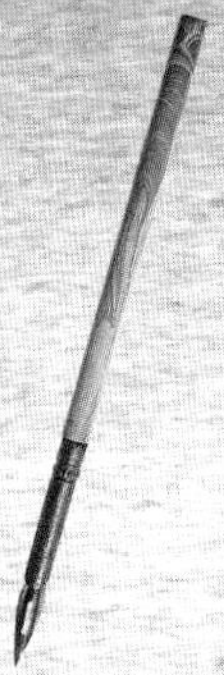

Published in Great Britain
in 2000 by Hodder Wayland,
an imprint of Hodder Children's Books

© Copyright 2000 Hodder Wayland

A catalogue record for this book is available from
the British Library.

ISBN 0 7502 2607 2

Printed and bound in Italy by G. Canale & C.Sp.A, Turin.

Hodder Children's Books
A division of Hodder Headline Limited
338 Euston Road, London, NW1 3BH

Cover and Decorative Pictures:
The cover shows a Victorian book, ink-well, pen, locket
and candle-holder, which can all be seen at the Museum
of London. The pictures that appear on the left-hand
pages of the book are a commemorative brooch from
Victoria's Diamond Jubilee (p. 4); an ink-well (p. 6, 10, 26);
a carnation (p. 8, 20, 28); a telescope (p. 12); an ink-pen
(p. 14, 22); a Peninsular War medal issued in 1848 (p. 16);
a locket containing a photograph and a lock of hair
(p. 18, 24). All objects are Victorian.

Picture Acknowledgements:
The publishers would like to thank the following for
permission to reproduce their pictures: Bridgeman Art
Library, London /Private Collection/Roger-Viollet, Paris 5
(bottom), /Private Collection 7 (top), 27 (top), 29 (top),
/Victoria & Albert Museum 9 (top), /Private Collection
/Christie's Images 9 (bottom), /Fitzwilliam Museum,
University of Cambridge 15 (top), /Walker Art Gallery,
Merseyside, UK (detail) 17 (top), /Bonhams, London 17
(bottom), 21 (right), /National Railway Museum, York 19
(bottom), /Central Saint Martins College of Art and
Design, London, UK 21 (left), /Royal Holloway and
Bedford New College, Surrey 23 (top), /The Crown Estate
29 (bottom); Girton College, Cambridge 25 (top); Hulton
Getty 5 (top), 7 (bottom), 23 (bottom); Mary Evans Picture
Library 11 (bottom); Museum of London *cover*, 3, 4, 6, 8,
10, 14, 18, 20, 22, 24, 26, 28; Natural History Museum,
London 11 (top); Peter Newark's Military Pictures 16;
Punch magazine 25 (bottom); Science Museum /Science
and Society Picture Library 12, 13, 15 (bottom), 19 (top),
27 (bottom).

CONTENTS

1897

Victoria

Mary Montgomerie Lamb (1843–1905)

Queen of so many nations that the sun
Sets not upon the boundaries of thy sway,
Whom men of varied clime and creed obey,
Mother of many princes, wife of one ...

How many glorious images unite
Round thine illustrious name!
The Dragon's head
Beneath St George's heel: the Lion's might:
Britannia: India's Empress, robed in red,
Crowned and enthroned! Then lo!
Thou com'st in sight,
A lonely woman, sable garmented.

(1887)

sway
Territory.

clime and creed
Climate and religion.
The poem is talking about
the many nationalities
ruled by Victoria.

Dragon,
St George, Lion
The symbols of Wales,
England and Scotland.

sable garmented
Dressed in black.

This is part of a sentimental poem written to commemorate the Golden Jubilee celebrations that marked Queen Victoria's fifty years of rule. It begins by describing the British Empire, which covers so much of the world that the sun never sets over all its lands at once. The images from different country's flags are united under Victoria, who represents Britannia – the female figure used as a symbol of Britain. But behind her powerful image Victoria is just an ordinary widow, dressed in 'sable', or black, to mourn her late husband Prince Albert.

Queen Victoria ruled the richest and most powerful country on earth for sixty-four years (1837–1901). No British monarch has reigned for longer. Events such as her Golden Jubilee were designed to be great festivals celebrating the might of Britain. As the focus of these occasions, Queen Victoria became a living symbol of the power and success of Britain.

Spectators pack the streets and rooftops as Victoria's Golden Jubilee parade passes through central London.

POET'S CORNER

Mary Montgomerie Lamb became a poet despite strong family disapproval. She published her earlier work under the name Violet Fane, to avoid offending her parents. As the wife of the British ambassador to the cities of Constantinople and then Rome, she would certainly have met the famous subject of her poem.

Britain's empire grew much larger during Victoria's reign. Many countries became British colonies, which means that they were taken over and controlled by Britain. Victoria was very proud of her empire. She described its function as being to 'protect the poor natives and advance civilization'. By the time Victoria died, in 1901, the British Empire covered a fifth of all the land on earth, and contained nearly a quarter of all the people in the world.

This magazine illustration from 1883 shows soldiers of many races, all fighting for Britain.

£300 a Year

Eliza Cook (1818–1889)

A housemaid, cook, and liveried boy
We must at once engage;
One of the two we must employ —
A footman or a page.

I cannot well resign at 'Lord's',
And you, dear Flo, of course
Must go to balls and make your calls
With decent brougham and horse.

Now, if I had three thousand, dear,
You know I would not hoard it;
But on three hundred pounds a year!
I really can't afford it.

liveried boy
A boy in servant's uniform.

footman, page
A butler's assistant, and a young errand-boy.

Lord's
A fashionable cricket club.

brougham
A covered, four-wheel carriage, with the driver's seat on the outside.

This is an extract from a poem about 'keeping up appearances'. It is a plea from a middle-class man to his fiancée. He describes the married lifestyle they would both like, but regrets that his income of £300 a year is not enough to pay for it. Eliza Cook came from a working-class background, but her poem shows that she knew all about middle-class attitudes. These lines struck a chord with Victorian readers, and this was one of her most popular poems.

Social class was very important to the Victorians, and Cook's poem lists the items necessary for people to consider themselves 'middle class'. They needed enough money for servants, society events, and a horse and carriage. It was considered wrong for a middle-class man to propose if he could not afford such things. Many couples married later in life, when the husband was earning a better salary.

Servants help this well-off family to enjoy Christmas, in an illustration from Pears Annual 1896.

The lives of most middle-class women revolved around visiting friends. For them, a small staff of servants was essential. New inventions such as vacuum cleaners, washing machines, electric irons and central heating were not widely used until late in Victorian times. Coal fires and gas lighting left a thin film of soot over every household surface. Endless scrubbing and polishing were needed to keep a house clean enough for guests.

Victorian servants like these lived more comfortable lives than most factory workers or miners.

POET'S CORNER

Eliza Cook was born in the working-class district of Southwark in London. She was the youngest of eleven children. Despite the poverty of her background she taught herself to read and write, and her work was published in literary magazines while she was still a teenager.

All Things Bright and Beautiful

Cecil Frances Humphreys Alexander (1818–1895)

All things bright and beautiful,
All creatures great and small,
All things wise and wonderful:
The Lord God made them all.

Each little flower that opens,
Each little bird that sings,
God made their glowing colours,
And made their tiny wings.

The rich man at his castle,
The poor man at his gate,
He made them high or lowly
And ordered their estate.

(1848)

high or lowly
Here, this means important or humble.

estate
Position in society.

This extract comes from the famous children's hymn celebrating the beauty of creation. The verse was inspired by a line from the Bible: 'And God saw everything that he had made, and, behold, it was very good' (Genesis 1:31). The hymn was first published in a book called *Hymns for Little Children*, where it was called *Maker of Heaven and Earth*. It was set to a tune called *Royal Oak*, which had been composed around 200 years earlier.

Thomas Webster's painting of a village choir shows people
dressed in their Sunday best for a church service.

POET'S CORNER

**Cecil Frances Humphreys
Alexander was the wife of
the Anglican Bishop of
Derry and Raphoe, in
Northern Ireland. She
wrote nearly 400 hymns,
including *There is a Green
Hill Far Away* and *Once in
Royal David's City*.**

During the Victorian era, fewer
people went to church than in
previous centuries (but still more than go
today). By the 1850s only one in three
people in England still attended regularly.
This was partly because working-class
people who laboured in factories only
had Sunday off. They used their precious
time to rest, or for leisure.

Many Victorians in the Church of
England saw nothing wrong with the
idea used in the third verse, that God
created a society of 'high or lowly', or
rich and poor. They thought that poverty
was God's will. Inside churches, rich
people sat on cushioned pews and knelt
to pray on padded rests. The poor of the
congregation sat on stools in the aisles,
and knelt to pray on the bare stone floor.

Henry Bacon's 1872 painting
Christmas Prayers *shows the pews
and prayer cushions of the wealthy
members of the congregation.*

9

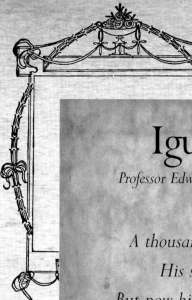

Iguanadon

Professor Edward Forbes (1815–1854)

A thousand ages underground
His skeleton has lain
But now his body's big and round
And he's himself again!

His bones, like Adam's wrapped in clay,
His ribs of iron stout,
Where is the brute alive today,
That dares with him turn out?

Beneath his hide he's got inside
The souls of living men
Who dare our Saurian now deride
With life in him again!

(1853)

Adam
According to Christian belief, God created the first man Adam from clay.

turn out
Fight.

Saurian
A scientific word for the dinosaur, meaning 'like a reptile'.

deride
Make fun of.

This poem was read to a group of scientists at a banquet on New Year's Eve, 1853. The banquet was held inside the life-size model of an iguanadon dinosaur, whose bones had recently been discovered. The poem describes how filling the model with lively scientists has brought the ancient dinosaur back to life. The scientists had not made the iguanadon model very accurately, however. The horn they put on its nose was in fact part of its thumb!

Professor Richard Owen holds the leg bone of a moa — an extinct ostrich-like bird from New Zealand.

Dinosaur bones were first discovered in England in the 1820s. The great Victorian scientist Professor Richard Owen — who was at the banquet — invented the word 'dinosaur' in 1841. He made the word up from two Greek words, *deinos* and *sauros*, meaning 'terrible reptile'. Life-size models of dinosaurs were displayed at Crystal Palace, to show the public what these strange creatures looked like.

In Victorian times, many people held strong Christian beliefs. They thought that the earth had been created in 4004 BC, and believed that all the creatures made by God were still in existence today. Church leaders were furious when scientists like Forbes and Owen claimed that dinosaurs had lived over 40 million years ago, and were now extinct. They would not have enjoyed hearing a poet compare the iguanadon to Adam.

POET'S CORNER

Iguanadon **was written by Edward Forbes, a highly respected naturalist. A newspaper reported that the audience cheered his poem like 'a herd of iguanadons'. Forbes spent much of his life studying molluscs and starfish. He died less than a year after the banquet.**

This 1854 engraving from the Illustrated London News *shows the banquet inside the iguanadon where Forbes read his poem.*

The Princess

Alfred, Lord Tennyson (1809–1892)

A man with knobs and wires and vials fired
A cannon: and here were telescopes
For azure views; and there a group of girls
In circle waited, whom the electric shock
Dislink'd with shrieks and laughter.

A dozen angry models jetted steam:
A petty railway ran: a fire-balloon
Rose gem-like up before the dusky groves
And dropped a fairy parachute and past:
And there thro' twenty posts of telegraph
They flash'd a saucy message to and fro.

(1847)

vials
Tubes full of liquid.

azure
Sky-blue.

Dislink'd
Unlinked – the shock broke their circle of held hands.

petty
Miniature, model.

gem-like
like a jewel.

past... thro'
Poetic ways of writing 'passed' and 'through'.

saucy
Light-hearted.

This extract comes from a poem describing a holiday fête arranged by a 'mechanics' institute' – a tradesmen's organization set up to educate its members and their families. Mechanical models, steam trains, the strange phenomenon of electricity, telegraph messages and other wonders of the Victorian era are being demonstrated. Tennyson describes them in a way that captures the excitement felt in an age of so many wonderful new inventions. He writes in 'blank' verse – with no rhymes. The pretty images and language contrast with the poem's serious scientific subject.

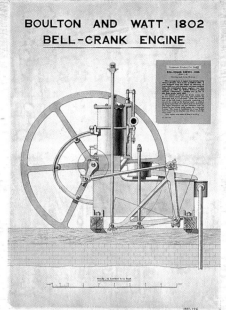

BOULTON AND WATT, 1802
BELL-CRANK ENGINE

An early nineteenth-century design for a steam engine. This engine could power a steam ship or drive factory machinery.

The Victorians were fascinated by scientific inventions. After all, they owed their success to inventions such as the steam engine. The machines in the new mills and factories, and the trains and ships that transported the goods they produced around the world, were all powered by steam engines. The scale of the Victorians' success was staggering. By the middle of the nineteenth century, Britain's factories were producing half the world's iron. Each worker in a cotton mill was producing as much material as 300 men would have done seventy years before.

During Victoria's reign, telegraph messages were first flashed from Britain to the USA, telephones were introduced (although the first London directory in 1880 contained barely 200 names), electricity was used to illuminate streets and houses, and images were first captured on photographic film.

POET'S CORNER

Alfred, Lord Tennyson was the most popular poet of the Victorian era. Born in Lincolnshire, his early life was troubled by poverty, the death of a close friend, and a family struck by alcoholism, drug abuse and madness. His most famous poems include *Idylls of the King* (about the legend of King Arthur), *The Lady of Shallott* and *In Memoriam*.

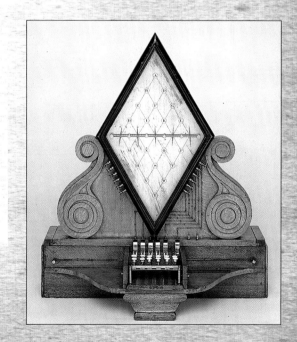

This beautiful device is one of the first telegraph machines ever made.

School Rhymes

An arithmetic textbook

Two pints will make one quart,
Four quarts will make one gallon strong.
Some drink too little, some too much,
To drink too much is wrong.

A sampler

The trees were green,
The sun was hot,
Sometimes I worked,
And sometimes not.
Seven years my age
My name Jane Grey
And often much
Too fond of play.

(Nineteenth Century)

pints
A pint was an old measurement equal to 0.568 litres.

quarts
A quart is equal to 1.136 litres.

gallon
A gallon is equal to 4.546 litres.

sampler
A detailed piece of embroidery made by a girl to show her sewing skills.

These simple rhymes can tell us a lot about the lives of Victorian schoolchildren. The first was chanted by a whole class, who would repeat it over and over. This was a popular way of teaching in Victorian schools. Children were often taught 'facts' (here, about measuring liquids), alongside 'morals' (about drinking alcohol). In the second rhyme, Jane Grey has been instructed, probably by her mother, to embroider a 'moral' message reminding her that she spends too much time enjoying herself, and not enough time making herself useful.

Victorian children's rhymes seem quaint to us, but their lives were very different. Many children had fathers who escaped from the hardships of working in factories by getting drunk. This makes the disapproving tone of the first rhyme quite easy to understand.

At the start of the nineteenth century, many poor children did not go to school. But by the end of Victoria's reign the government had introduced compulsory education for all children up to the age of twelve. Lessons were known as the 'three Rs': Reading, wRiting and aRithmetic! Badly trained, poorly paid teachers often relied on the cane to make their pupils behave. Another rhyme from the playground went: 'Georgie Ware is a very good man/ He teaches his children all he can/ To read and write and arithmetic/ And don't forget to give them the stick.'

This elaborate Victorian sampler, made from wool and silk, displays the words of a hymn.

These children in a primary school are practising their writing.

POET'S CORNER

Poor Jane Grey, only seven years old, confesses to not doing enough with her life. In Victorian times many children died young. In Liverpool in the 1840s, for example, fifty per cent of all children died before they were five. Perhaps Jane's mother was right to wonder if her daughter should be packing more into her little life.

Vitai Lampada
(The Torch of Life)

Sir Henry Newbolt (1862–1938)

There's a breathless hush in the close tonight —
Ten to make and the match to win —
A bumping pitch and a blinding light,
An hour to play and the last man in.
And it's not for the sake of a ribboned coat,
Or the selfish hope of a season's fame,
But his captain's hand on his shoulder smote —
'Play up! play up! and play the game!'

(1897)

close
A school playing-field.

ribboned coat
A coat decorated with the medals of a war hero.

smote
Struck. The captain is patting the player on the shoulder.

This first verse of a famous moral poem describes a school cricket match in heroic terms. Even the Latin title sounds important. The team's last batsman is in a difficult situation, but he is inspired by loyalty to his team, rather than by any selfish thrill of winning. The poem's next verse shows its hero at war in a more serious predicament – 'The Gatling's jammed and the Colonel dead'. But again he urges his troops to 'Play up! play up! and play the game!'. This captures perfectly the Victorian belief that wars, like cricket matches, could be won through the noble traditions of honour and fair play.

Old soldiers in 1875. They wear the 'ribboned coats' that record the bravery they showed in some of the many battles fought during Victoria's reign.

POET'S CORNER

Henry Newbolt was famous for his patriotic poems, celebrating the British Empire. *Vitai Lampada* became a great favourite among pupils at public schools. Newbolt was a friend of Field Marshall Douglas Haig, who was Britain's commander-in-chief during the First World War.

Shortly before Victoria came to the throne, the headmasters of public schools began to think that perhaps team sports might teach their pupils loyalty, co-operation, and self-control. Many of the games we know today, such as football, cricket, rugby, tennis and athletics, developed their modern rules and styles in Victorian times. Because working-class people worked from Monday to Saturday, sport remained mainly a pastime of the middle or upper classes – until factories began closing on Saturday afternoons.

Poems like *Vitai Lampada* were learnt by heart, and they helped to make ideas of fair play and sportsmanship popular. The Victorians had a romantic view of sport and war. A battle was described similarly to a cricket match. The horrors of the First World War would change such attitudes for ever.

A cricket match at a Victorian public school. Sports such as football, rugby and cricket gradually spread from upper-class schools like this one, to the rest of society.

From a Railway Carriage

Robert Louis Stevenson (1850–1894)

Faster than fairies, faster than witches,
Bridges and houses, hedges and ditches;
And charging along like troops in a battle,
All through the meadows the horses and cattle;
All of the sights of the hill and the plain
Fly as thick as driving rain;
And ever again, in the wink of an eye,
Painted stations whistled by.

... here is a cart run away in the road
Lumping along with man and load;
And here is a mill and there is a river;
Each a glimpse and gone for ever!

(1885)

Lumping

*Moving in a clumsy way.
Stevenson is comparing
the old-fashioned horse
and cart to the
modern railway.*

With its tumbling verses and breathless pace, this extract cleverly captures the head-over-heels excitement of speeding through the countryside aboard a steam train. The rhythm of the verse imitates the 'clickety-clack' rhythm of the train's wheels. In our age of motorway travel and jet planes, it is difficult to imagine how thrilling it must have been to travel by train for the first time. Before the invention of the locomotive, the fastest anyone had travelled was on the back of a horse.

Railways were an ingenious combination of two previous inventions – steam engines, which were used in factories; and grooved wheels running on rails, which were used in mining. The first railway engine, Richard Trevethick's *Locomotion No. 1*, was built at the start of the century, and was hailed by the *Observer* newspaper as 'the most astonishing machine ever invented'.

George Earl's 1895 painting
Perth Station, Coming South
shows the bustle and excitement of
travelling on Victorian railways.

POET'S CORNER

Robert Louis Stevenson wrote several of the Victorian era's most popular books. His novels include *The Strange Case of Dr Jekyll and Mr Hyde, Kidnapped,* and *Treasure Island* with its famous pirate Long John Silver. This poem comes from *A Child's Garden of Verses,* in which Stevenson writes about memories of his childhood.

The railways transformed the country. Steam trains transported factory goods faster and more cheaply than road or canal. As the cost of taking produce from farm to city dropped, so food became less expensive. Cheap train fares meant that ordinary people could afford to travel, and trips to the seaside became popular. Towns such as Brighton and Blackpool now attracted visitors by building promenades, theatres and amusement arcades.

Cheap train fares meant that
poor people could now afford to travel
by train – though not always
in great comfort!

If it Wasn't for the 'Ouses in Between

Edgar Bateman

If you saw my little backyard,
'Wot a pretty spot!' you'd cry,
It's a picture on a sunny summer day;
Wiv the turnip tops and cabbages
wot peoples doesn't buy
I makes it on a Sunday look all gay.
The neighbours finks I grow 'em
and you'd fancy you're in Kent,
Or at Epsom if you gaze into the mews.
It's a wonder as the landlord
doesn't want to raise the rent,
Because we've got such nobby distant views.

Oh it really is a wery pretty garden
And Chingford to the eastward could be seen;
Wiv a ladder and some glasses,
You could see to 'Ackney Marshes,
If it wasn't for the 'ouses in between.

(1894)

This famous comic song was sung in 'music hall', a popular Victorian form of entertainment. It is written in the slang, or 'colloquial', voice of a working-class Londoner, who is singing about his new home. He has made enough money to move from a crowded slum in central London, to a new house in the suburbs with its own backyard. The joke is that even here, the view the singer is so proud of is spoilt by all the other houses!

mews
A row of stables, often converted into houses.

nobby
Smart; something that a wealthy person or 'nob' might have.

Chingford
A suburb of north-east London.

glasses
Binoculars.

'Ackney Marshes
Hackney Marshes is a large stretch of undeveloped land that was too boggy to build on.

Music hall, which featured singers, dancers and variety acts, played to packed theatres. Edgar Bateman was one of its most successful comic songwriters. He was known as 'The Shakespeare of Aldgate Pump' because of the working-class area of London he lived in. He wrote *The 'Ouses in Between* for popular cockney singer Gus Elen.

This engraving from 1872 shows the crowded conditions of terraced housing in London.

Between 1800 and 1900, London became the largest city in the world. The population grew from one million to four-and-a-half million. Wealthy people lived in fashionable west London in big houses, but the poor were crammed into appalling slums in the east.

In the 1850s, horse-drawn 'omnibuses' and the new railways made it possible for poorer people to move away from the slums and travel to the city centre each day to work. In the suburbs, row upon row of identical houses like the one described in the poem were built. Many were small two-storey terraces, with a tiny garden and an outside toilet. But to those people who had moved from the stinking, teeming slums, the new houses must have seemed luxurious.

Urchins in a gloomy London street. St Paul's Cathedral can be seen at the end of the alley.

The Song of the Shirt

Thomas Hood (1799–1845)

With fingers weary and worn,
With eyelids heavy and red
A woman sat, in unwomanly rags,
Plying her needle and thread —
Stitch! Stitch! Stitch!
In poverty, hunger and dirt,
And stiff with dolorous pitch
She sang the 'Song of the Shirt'.

Work — work — work!
My labour never flags;
And what are its wages? A bed of straw,
A crust of bread — and rags.

(1843)

unwomanly
Not showing the appearance of a woman.

Plying
Using or working with.

dolorous pitch
Miserable tone. She is singing in a low, sad voice.

flags
Becomes slower.

This is an extract from a poem about a seamstress – a woman who makes clothes for a living. It was inspired by the true story of a widow with two children, who earned 35 pence a week making trousers for 7 pence a pair. The poem continues: 'Oh, God that bread should be so dear, and flesh and blood so cheap!' Its heavy, plodding rhythm and repetition of words imitate the endless and unchanging work of the unhappy seamstress.

This famous painting from 1874 shows poor people queuing up for medical treatment.

A cartoon from the magazine Punch. *The workers in a sweatshop look like skeletons, while their boss grows fat.*

POET'S CORNER

Only in his forties did Thomas Hood begin writing about social injustices. Originally published in *Punch* magazine's Christmas edition, his *Song of the Shirt* had an immediate impact. It was reprinted in *The Times* and other newspapers, translated into French, German, Italian and Russian, printed on leaflets and handkerchiefs, and turned into a play.

During the nineteenth century, Britain became the richest nation on earth. But many Victorian workers, like the seamstress in the poem, faced a life of terrible hardship. They worked almost every hour they were awake, to earn just enough money to keep themselves and their families from starving.

The clothing industry was one of the most successful in Victoria's reign. Cotton clothes, which were light to wear and easy to wash and dye, were very popular. There was a huge market overseas, especially in hot lands such as India which had become part of the British Empire. Clothes were made by individuals working alone at home, or in small factories known as sweat-shops. These were badly lit and poorly ventilated. Such conditions frequently caused blindness and fatal illnesses.

A Girton Girl

Catherine Grant Furley

When you met me first, at dinner,
At the hall the other night,
You were seated on my left hand,
The professor on my right.

And you saw I cared to listen —
Saw it with scornful mirth —
To the facts that he was telling,
Of the strata of the earth.

'Tis you who err, believe me,
Thinking, as perchance you do,
That because her brain is empty,
Woman's heart must beat more true.

(1887)

hall
A university building.

scornful mirth
Mocking laughter.

strata
Layers of rock under the earth's surface.

err
Make a mistake.

perchance
Perhaps.

These words reveal the secret thoughts of a young woman studying at Girton College, Cambridge – the first university college for women. She is worried that a man she meets at dinner finds her less attractive (and indeed laughs at her) because she is clever. She uses the poem to tell him that her interest in geology (and in other subjects once thought too scientific for women to understand), does not make her any less feminine.

The 1898 Girton Cricket team. These women were among the first in Britain to be educated at university

Throughout history, women have been seen as homemakers and mothers. In Victorian times, though, attitudes began to change. Some women began to feel that they should be treated as men's equals, and that a good education was the best way to achieve this. The opening of Girton College in 1869 was a major breakthrough.

Many Victorians felt that education was wasted on women. Some medical experts even claimed that strenuous study would make women unable to have children! Queen Victoria herself criticized 'the mad folly of Women's Rights'. She said that a woman 'would become the most hateful, heartless and disgusting human ... were she allowed to unsex herself'. Perhaps her words haunted Catherine Grant Furley. Later in her poem, she writes: ' 'tis not learning that unsexes.'

In this cartoon from Punch, women students prefer the company of their elderly professors — to the disappointment of the younger male students.

25

May Day Ode

William Makepeace Thackeray (1811–1863)

Sheltered by crystal wall and roof, we view

All products of the earth, the air, and seas,

Assuming every texture, form and hue,

That can a man's corporeal senses please,

And gladden beauty's sense to ecstasies ...

(1851)

Assuming
Taking the appearance of.

hue
Colour.

corporeal senses
Physical feelings.

ecstasies
Great happiness.

The Millennium Dome is not such a new idea.
Between 1 May ('May Day') and October 1851, the
most extraordinary exhibition the world had ever seen was held
in Hyde Park, London. It was called the Great Exhibition, and
took place inside the Crystal Palace – a glass hall three times
the length of St Paul's Cathedral. Some 13,000 exhibits from
around the world demonstrated the latest wonders of science,
medicine, technology and industry. This poem uses majestic,
flowery language, as Thackeray tries somehow to put into
words the overwhelming size and variety of the exhibition,
and the almost religious wonder it inspired in him.

POET'S CORNER

William Makepeace Thackeray is less known for his poetry than for novels such as *Vanity Fair*. After dropping out of Cambridge and studying art in Paris, Thackeray became a successful journalist. He wrote for both *Punch* and *The Times*, and was a keen observer of London society. So, the Great Exhibition would have held a special interest for him.

Queen Victoria and Prince Albert arrive to open the Great Exhibition, on May Day 1851.

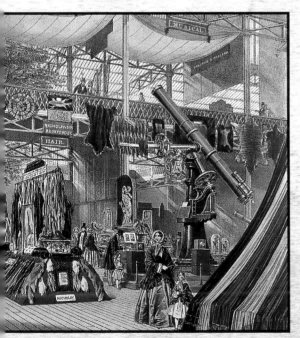

Inside the Crystal Palace, visitors admire furs and skins from around the British Empire.

Thackeray was one of many poets inspired to write about the Great Exhibition in such awestruck tones. Another poet, John Davidson, described it as 'our very own eighth wonder of the world'. Inspired by Queen Victoria's husband, Prince Albert, the Great Exhibition was visited by over six million people – at least one in five of the population.

Exhibits such as huge, noisy steam engines and locomotives, massive factory machines, and a working telegraph link to Manchester and Edinburgh enthralled the 25,000 people who came every day. It left no visitor in doubt that Britain was the most advanced, wealthy and ingenious nation on earth. The Queen herself was said to have visited thirty times. After one visit she wrote in her diary: 'We are capable of doing anything.'

27

WAR

The Charge of the Light Brigade

Alfred, Lord Tennyson (1809–1892)

Half a league, half a league
Half a league onward,
All in the valley of Death
Rode the six hundred.
'Forward the Light Brigade!
Charge for the guns!' he said:
Into the valley of Death
Rode the six hundred.

'Forward the Light Brigade!'
Was there a man dismay'd?
Not tho' the soldier knew
Some one had blunder'd:
Their's not to make reply,
Their's not to reason why,
Their's but to do and die:
Into the valley of Death
Rode the six hundred.

(1854)

league
An old measure of length, roughly equivalent to 2.2 km.

Light Brigade
A regiment of lightly armed soldiers who fought on horseback.

dismay'd
Dismayed — losing strength and courage through fear.

tho'
Short for 'though'.

blunder'd
Blundered — made a stupid mistake.

This poem honours the great courage of British soldiers in the Crimean War (1853–56). During the Battle of Balaclava, 673 British cavalrymen recklessly charged into Russian cannons at one end of a valley. The relentless rhythm of the poem suggests the thunder of their horses' hooves. Nearly 250 men of the Light Brigade were killed. Their tragic fate is captured with an echo of *Psalm 23*: 'Yea, though I walk through the valley of the shadow of death, I will fear no evil.'

The heroic charge of the Light Brigade captured the imagination of Europe. This painting of the tragic incident hangs in a gallery in Madrid.

POET'S CORNER

Tennyson wrote this poem after he succeeded William Wordsworth as the Poet Laureate in 1850. He was inspired by reports of the incident in *The Times*. It is one of his most famous poems, and became popular with British soldiers in the Crimea. Tennyson even arranged for 2,000 copies to be sent out to them.

The Crimean War was fought by Britain, France and Turkey against Russia. It was the first war Britain had fought for forty years, and was seen by many Victorians as a glorious adventure. News reports from journalists in the Crimea soon painted a very different picture. The troops were badly led and poorly equipped. The heroism described by Tennyson came at a terrible cost.

Muddled orders ('Some one had blunder'd') caused the Light Brigade's commander, Lord Cardigan, to lead his men into the path of the Russian guns. Cardigan was not popular with his soldiers. He was a haughty, rich aristocrat, who had travelled to the Crimea in his own yacht! But when Cardigan returned home, the newspaper reports and Tennyson's poem had turned him into a national hero.

This marble bust of Lord Cardigan perfectly captures the arrogance and pride of an aristocratic Victorian officer.

GLOSSARY

Difficult words from the verse appear alongside each poem. This glossary explains words used in the main text. The page numbers are given so that you can study the glossary then see how the words have been used.

ambassador (p. 5) An official representing his monarch or government in a foreign country.

Anglican (p. 9) A religion developed from the Church of England.

aristocrat (p. 29) Someone belonging to the top rank of the upper classes.

awestruck (p. 27) Filled with wonder.

blank verse (p. 12) Poetry which does not use rhyme.

Britannia (p. 4) The figure of a woman with helmet, shield and trident, used as a symbol of Britain.

British Empire (p. 4) Countries around the world ruled over by the British monarch.

canal (p. 19) A man-made river.

cockney (p. 21) Someone from the East End of London, often speaking a special slang.

commemorate (p. 4) Do or write something to celebrate and remember a special event.

compulsory (p. 15) Enforced, having to be done.

congregation (p. 9) The group of people attending a church service.

extinct (p. 11) No longer in existence (for example, species of animal that have died out).

extract (p. 8) Part of a poem or story.

folly (p. 25) Foolishness.

geology (p. 24) The study of the structure of the earth.

Golden Jubilee (p. 5) The celebration of a monarch ruling for fifty years.

haughty (p. 29) Thinking of yourself as better than others.

illuminate (p. 13) Light up.

ingenious (p. 19) Very clever and inventive.

injustices (p. 23) Acts or situations which are unfair to certain people.

Latin (p. 16) The language introduced by the ancient Romans, and used for classical texts.

locomotive (p. 18) An engine which moves under its own power, especially the part of a train that pulls the carriages.

majestic (p. 26) Grand, imposing, stately.

middle class (p. 7) The class of society between the upper and working classes, including professional and business workers and their families.

molluscs (p. 11) A class of animals including shellfish and snails.

monarch (p. 5) A king or queen.

morals (p. 14) Ideas of right and wrong, and of good and bad behaviour.

natives (p. 5) Local inhabitants of a country.

naturalist (p. 11) A scientist who studies animals and plants.

noble (p. 16) Decent, admirable, unselfish.

omnibuses (p. 21) This is the proper word for buses.

overwhelming *(p. 26) Creating so much emotion that it cannot be expressed.*

patriotic *(p. 17) Being very proud of your country.*

pews *(p. 9) Seats in a church.*

phenomenon *(p. 12) An extraordinary person, thing or event.*

Poet Laureate *(p. 29) The poet appointed by the monarch to write poems celebrating important State occasions.*

promenades *(p. 19) Paved, public walkways at the seaside.*

public schools *(p. 17) Schools usually attended only by children from the upper classes and middle classes, whose parents have to pay fees.*

reptile *(p. 11) A class of animals including crocodiles, lizards, snakes, tortoises and turtles.*

sentimental *(p. 4) Affected by feelings and emotions.*

slum *(p. 20) Overcrowded, unhealthy housing for the poor in a city.*

soot *(p. 7) A fine, black dust created by burning wood, coal, oil or gas.*

steam engines *(p. 19) Machines that use steam to create power.*

strenuous *(p. 25) Energetic, tiring.*

suburbs *(p. 20) The district on the outskirts of a city.*

telegraph *(p. 13) An electrical device for transmitting messages over long distances.*

tradesmen *(p. 12) Craftsmen and shopkeepers.*

unsex *(p. 25) Deprive someone of certain qualities believed to be suitable to their sex.*

variety acts *(p. 21) Singers, dancers, comedians and novelty performers.*

ventilated *(p. 23) Allowing fresh air to enter.*

working class *(p. 6) The class of a society that provides the manual and industrial labourers, and usually contains the poorest people.*

BOOKS TO READ

Victorian England as seen by Punch by Frank E. Huggett (Sidgwick and Jackson, 1978)

Victorians by Margaret Sharman (Evans Brothers Ltd, 1995)

Victorian Britain by Andrew Langley (Hamlyn, 1994)

The Penguin Book of Victorian Verse by Daniel Karlin (editor) (The Penguin Press, 1997)

The Penguin Book of Everyday Verse, Social and Documentary Poetry 1250–1916 by David Wright (editor) (Penguin Books Ltd, 1976)

Learning and Teaching in Victorian Times by P. F. Speed (Longman, 1988)

INDEX

Numbers in **bold** refer
to pictures and captions.